Two Years in the "Wild West"

A long time ago there was a German prince and a Swiss painter who set sail from Holland on an extraordinary journey to America. The year was 1832 and the prince's name was Maximilian of Wied. The artist who went with him on this exciting expedition was called Karl Bodmer, and these are some of the pictures that he painted during his travels. The two friends were setting out on a thrilling adventure which was to take them right across North America. They made their way slowly through the country inhabited by the Native Americans—a territory which was still unknown to many at that time. The prairieland stretched from the "father of all rivers", the Mississippi, in the east, to the imposing Rocky Mountains in the west, and from central Canada in the north to the border with Mexico along the Rio Grande in the south. Wherever he went, Karl Bodmer sketched and painted the chiefs, medicine men, dancers and warriors of the tribes on the Great Plains, capturing in pencil and watercolor the daily life of the Native Americans, the countryside, and the animals which roamed the area. Bodmer's pictures immortalized life in the "Wild West" for future generations.

Let him carry us off to a world of daring buffalo hunters and skilled riders . . .

3

Up and Away In No Time

The tribes of North America's western Great Plains were skilled horsemen who lived in tepees, tent-like dwellings with a conical framework of slender poles. They were nomads, which means that they never settled in one place, since the tribes followed migrating buffalo herds as they moved across the plains. The Native Americans had to be able to set up and take down their camps quickly and easily—a task that was carried out by the women. Two women required half an hour for one tepee. First of all, they would fix four equally spaced wooden poles in the ground, and then bind them together at the top. Next, they would strengthen this framework by adding another dozen or so poles and by covering them with buffalo hides that had been sewn together. The entrance to the tepees always faced east, for the Native Americans believed that the light of the morning sun brought wisdom. This also prevented the westerly winds from blowing through the front flap. As long as the flap was open, visitors were welcome to enter, however, if it was shut, they would have to wait until invited in. The painted animals on the outside of the tepees related stories about the bravery and skillful deeds of the owner, and it was also believed that these animals would help protect those inside against illness and misfortune.

4

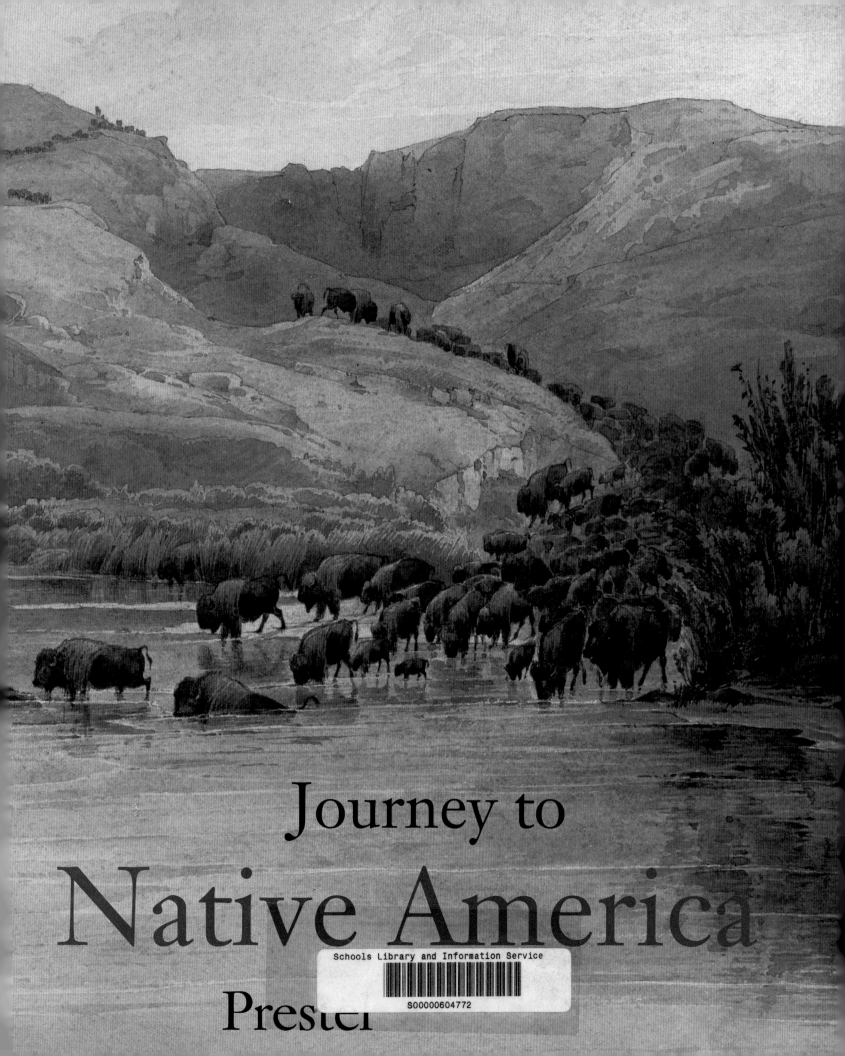

Journey to
Native America

Prestel

Böhrok-ohk-cha-te — den 9ᵗᵉⁿ April 1834

Fort Mandan.

Life in an Earth Lodge Village

Not all tribes lived in tepees. Those Native Americans inhabiting the eastern territory of the Great Plains lived in large, dome-shaped dwellings known as earth lodges, which were partly hidden from sight in the ground. From a distance they looked like mounds of earth scooped up from the surrounding area. These earth dwellings were built around four heavy wooden posts joined together by connecting beams. The arched cavern was then formed by covering a number of smaller posts with willow rods, grass and earth and a large hole in the roof was left in the middle over the fire pit to let out the smoke and let in the light. During the summer months it was pleasantly cool inside, while it remained warm and snug in the wintertime. Between thirty and forty people could fit comfortably into an earth lodge and there was even enough room for the owner's horses so that they could keep warm too!

Work and Play

The children on the Plains were raised as members of one big family. They used to run around wherever they wanted to, play games, and get up to all sorts of tricks, without really ever being told off. Parents or other relatives would tell the children about all the things that had to be done and what was expected of them. If ever the children began to get out of hand, cold water was simply poured over their heads to cool them down! Boys and girls were prepared for life as grown-ups at a very young age. Sons would go along with their fathers on hunting expeditions, when they would learn how to catch fish and hunt rabbits. Daughters would stay behind at camp to help their mothers, who taught them how to cook, tan hides and carry out other domestic work. The tepees were looked after by the women, and it was the women who

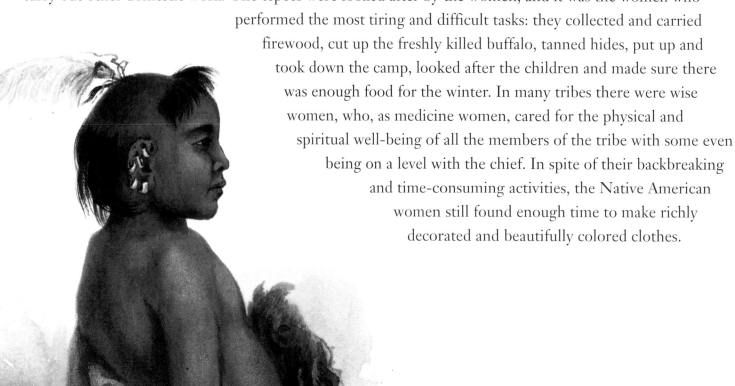

performed the most tiring and difficult tasks: they collected and carried firewood, cut up the freshly killed buffalo, tanned hides, put up and took down the camp, looked after the children and made sure there was enough food for the winter. In many tribes there were wise women, who, as medicine women, cared for the physical and spiritual well-being of all the members of the tribe with some even being on a level with the chief. In spite of their backbreaking and time-consuming activities, the Native American women still found enough time to make richly decorated and beautifully colored clothes.

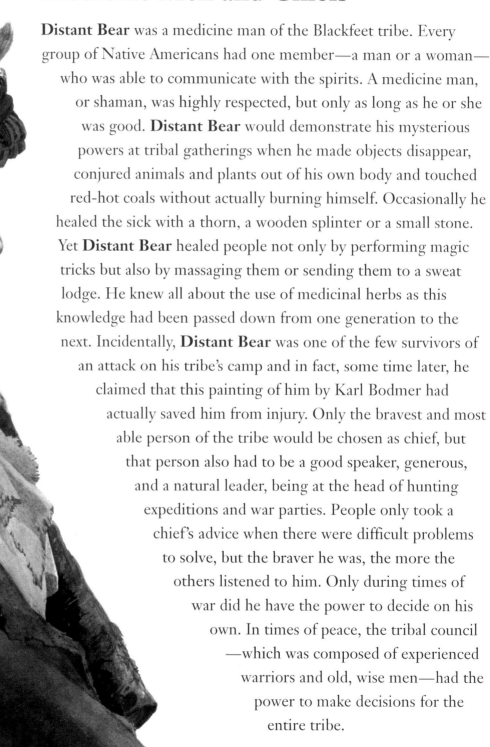

Medicine Men and Chiefs

Distant Bear was a medicine man of the Blackfeet tribe. Every group of Native Americans had one member—a man or a woman—who was able to communicate with the spirits. A medicine man, or shaman, was highly respected, but only as long as he or she was good. **Distant Bear** would demonstrate his mysterious powers at tribal gatherings when he made objects disappear, conjured animals and plants out of his own body and touched red-hot coals without actually burning himself. Occasionally he healed the sick with a thorn, a wooden splinter or a small stone. Yet **Distant Bear** healed people not only by performing magic tricks but also by massaging them or sending them to a sweat lodge. He knew all about the use of medicinal herbs as this knowledge had been passed down from one generation to the next. Incidentally, **Distant Bear** was one of the few survivors of an attack on his tribe's camp and in fact, some time later, he claimed that this painting of him by Karl Bodmer had actually saved him from injury. Only the bravest and most able person of the tribe would be chosen as chief, but that person also had to be a good speaker, generous, and a natural leader, being at the head of hunting expeditions and war parties. People only took a chief's advice when there were difficult problems to solve, but the braver he was, the more the others listened to him. Only during times of war did he have the power to decide on his own. In times of peace, the tribal council —which was composed of experienced warriors and old, wise men—had the power to make decisions for the entire tribe.

Chief **Maker of Roads,** who Karl Bodmer painted here, was an important chief of the Hidatsa Native Americans. He had led his people to war six times in a row, without having lost a single man.

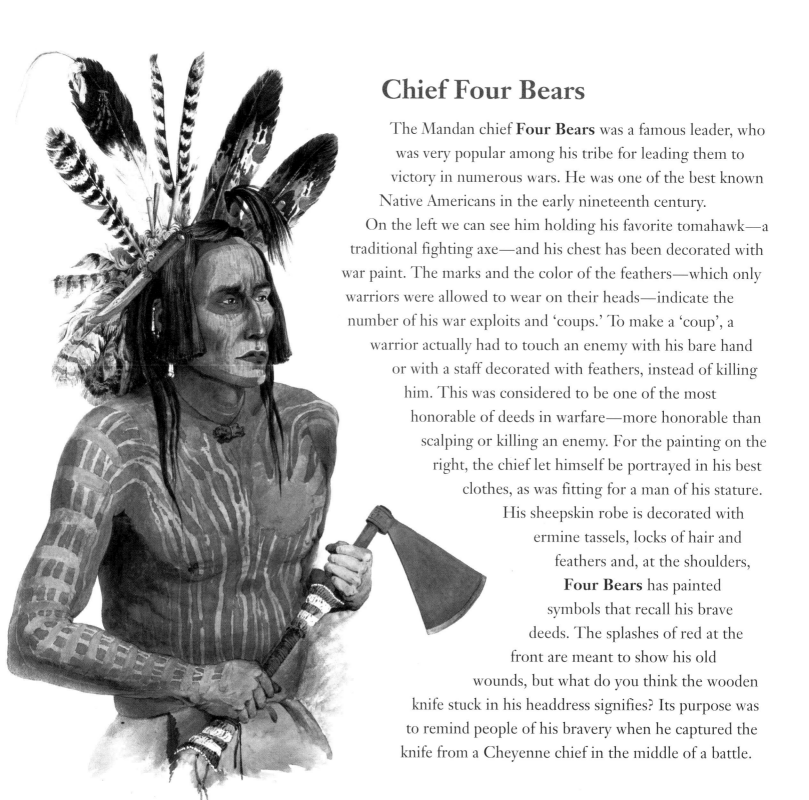

Chief Four Bears

The Mandan chief **Four Bears** was a famous leader, who was very popular among his tribe for leading them to victory in numerous wars. He was one of the best known Native Americans in the early nineteenth century.

On the left we can see him holding his favorite tomahawk—a traditional fighting axe—and his chest has been decorated with war paint. The marks and the color of the feathers—which only warriors were allowed to wear on their heads—indicate the number of his war exploits and 'coups.' To make a 'coup', a warrior actually had to touch an enemy with his bare hand or with a staff decorated with feathers, instead of killing him. This was considered to be one of the most honorable of deeds in warfare—more honorable than scalping or killing an enemy. For the painting on the right, the chief let himself be portrayed in his best clothes, as was fitting for a man of his stature. His sheepskin robe is decorated with ermine tassels, locks of hair and feathers and, at the shoulders, **Four Bears** has painted symbols that recall his brave deeds. The splashes of red at the front are meant to show his old wounds, but what do you think the wooden knife stuck in his headdress signifies? Its purpose was to remind people of his bravery when he captured the knife from a Cheyenne chief in the middle of a battle.

12

On the Warpath

Chief **Fours Bears** and all his friends usually attacked other tribes either because of long-standing disagreements or because they wanted to steal the other tribe's horses. Every man could decide for himself if he wanted to fight or not, but this was often seen as a chance for the men to show how brave and powerful they were and to earn highly-prized feathers for their headdresses. Warriors would begin preparations by painting their faces and bodies, which was a way of asking the spirits to let them return safely to their village. Then the 'peace pipe' they used to smoke together would be broken into hundreds of little pieces.

After this declaration of war, between thirty and fifty warriors would set off for battle. In single file, each tried to walk in the footsteps of the man in front of him (which has now given us the word 'warpath'). In this way, they moved quietly through enemy territory, hoping that they would not be seen. It also made it impossible for the enemy to guess how many warriors were on the warpath. Attacks generally occurred at dawn and usually took no longer than a few minutes. Accompanied by the sound of piercing screams, the warriors charged down on the enemy's camp. They would steal horses and even drag away prisoners, who would often be kept hostage by the victorious tribe. Karl Bodmer captured such a scene in this exciting picture. While he was drawing, Prince Maximilian and the others from the fort assisted their friends from the Blackfeet tribe in a fight against the Cree and Assiniboin tribes.

Grass-Eating Dogs and Harvest Mice

In the middle of the seventeenth century, the Native Americans of the Plains discovered wild horses roaming the vast grasslands. Since these animals reminded them of their pets, they called them 'grass-eating dogs.' These horses were descendants of those brought to the southwest by the Spaniards, and the tribes people soon recognized how useful these creatures—which were also known as mustangs—could be. They tamed them and rode them without saddles or reins; they would urge the horses on with their knees and heels, guiding them with a simple leather slip-noose fitted over the horse's lower jaw. The inhabitants of the Plains were considered to be among the finest, most skilled riders in the world.

The Native Americans regarded all animals, even the smallest ones, as gifts provided by Mother Nature, and they treated them with the utmost care and respect. Take the little harvest mouse, for example: the Native Americans of the Plains treasured the beans of a special plant that grew locally. However, the beans were very difficult to harvest because they grew beneath the grass-covered ground and were hard to find. But, as its name suggests, the Harvest Mouse had an easier time of it. To be able to survive the cold winter months, these mice used to collect hundreds of beans and store them in their holes underground. The Native Americans simply dug down into these holes and took half the beans and, in their place, they would leave some corn and buffalo fat as a way of saying 'thank-you.'

Buffalo and Other Basics

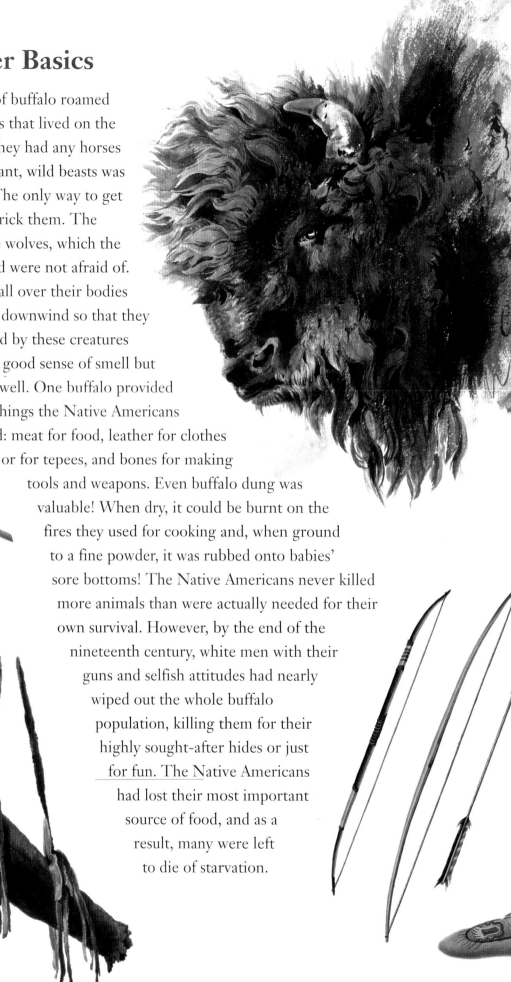

In springtime, when millions of buffalo roamed across the grasslands, the tribes that lived on the Plains set off to hunt. Before they had any horses to help them, hunting these giant, wild beasts was very difficult and dangerous. The only way to get near the buffalo was to try to trick them. The hunters dressed up to look like wolves, which the buffalo were used to seeing and were not afraid of. They also smeared buffalo fat all over their bodies and approached the herds downwind so that they would not be noticed by these creatures which have a very good sense of smell but do not see very well. One buffalo provided many of the things the Native Americans needed: meat for food, leather for clothes or for tepees, and bones for making tools and weapons. Even buffalo dung was valuable! When dry, it could be burnt on the fires they used for cooking and, when ground to a fine powder, it was rubbed onto babies' sore bottoms! The Native Americans never killed more animals than were actually needed for their own survival. However, by the end of the nineteenth century, white men with their guns and selfish attitudes had nearly wiped out the whole buffalo population, killing them for their highly sought-after hides or just for fun. The Native Americans had lost their most important source of food, and as a result, many were left to die of starvation.

18

When the  Buffalo Dances

Dancing always played an important part in Native American rituals, and was integral to the day-
to-day life of all tribes. In colorful ceremonies of song and dance, they gave thanks to the spirits
and asked for their help and protection. This was done before a hunt or at the outbreak of war,
at victory celebrations, the start of a new season, or when a member of the tribe died.
One of the most famous dances was called 'Buffalo Come,' and was performed by the Native
Americans of the Plains. The dancers dressed up in buffalo masks and, waving weapons above their
heads, hoped to lure the buffalo herds as close to the village as possible. With threatening drum
rhythms, deafening rattling noises and a monotone chant, they would dance until the scouts—
tribesmen who had left the camp to look for the animals—caught sight of the first buffalo. But
just imagine: this could take several days and nights!

The Buffalo Bull Society

To the left we can see one of the 'Buffalo Bull Society' dancers. One of the functions of the society was to ensure that certain rules were observed during the buffalo hunt and afterwards when the beast was divided up amongst the hunters. Belonging to a society was very important to the Native Americans. First of all, young men joined the 'Society of Foolish Dogs,' and only later, when they were grown-up, were they allowed to become members of the honorable 'Buffalo Bull Society,' by paying a 'fee' of either one horse or a specially made blanket.

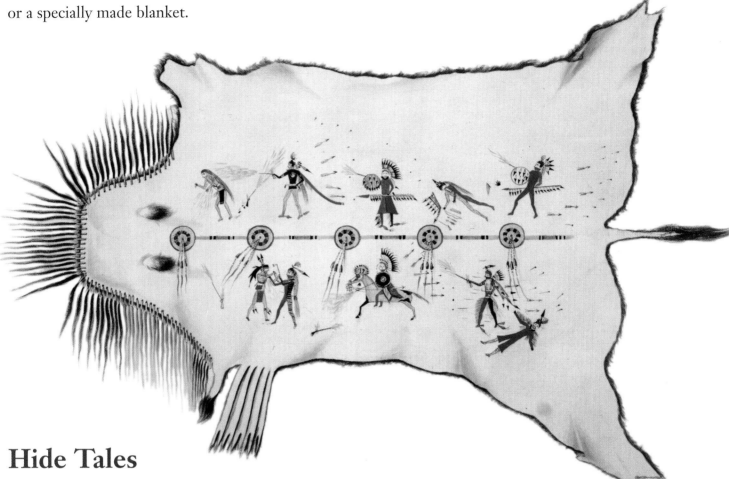

Hide Tales

On special occasions the chiefs of Native American tribes who lived on the Plains wore garments made of ornately decorated buffalo hides. The patterns and pictures could only be seen clearly in winter when they wore the fur on the inside to keep them warm. In summer, they then turned the skins inside out. Chief **Four Bears**—who we met earlier—was not only a leader but also a talented artist. The scenes he depicted with a sharp piece of wood on his buffalo robe tell of one of the many raids he led. At the lower left, for example, you can see him in combat with a Cheyenne chief. **Four Bears** is shown wielding his tomahawk while grabbing his enemy's knife, and the red paint reveals that he injured his hand in the fight.

The colors used in such paintings came from animals, plants or minerals. Much finer shades can be produced with these natural colors than with today's chemically produced ones. The Blackfeet Native Americans, for example, knew how to make half a dozen red tones from different types of soil and from the bud of the pussy willow.

Where the Spirits Roam

Native Americans grew up believing there were mysterious forces at work in nature, which had powers much greater than those on Earth. Spirits colored the rainbows and blotted out the sun to make eclipses. Every young man had to be close to these natural powers so that he could come face to face with his protective spirit on what was called a 'vision quest.' Only those who had found their protective spirit were allowed to include themselves among the elders and to take part in war parties.

Wearing only a loincloth and equipped with a pipe, tobacco, and a blanket, a young man would set off to find his protective spirit. He would head for a mountain peak, a spot in a hot desert, or a holy and mysterious place where he would rest, without eating anything, for four days. His hunger and thirst would cause intensive dreams or visions, and if for example a buffalo appeared in his dream, it would then become his very own protective spirit. From then on, he would carry a buffalo hoof or horn with him wherever he went. If he saw an eagle, an eagle's wing or a claw would become his lucky charm.

26

The Eternal Hunting Grounds

Many Native Americans believed in life after death. When a member of their tribe died, the others went into mourning as a sign of respect for the dead person, but at the same time, they would have a celebration. They believed the spirits of the dead went to a better world: a paradise where mighty buffalo herds were thought to roam vast prairies, covering the area with a carpet of black, and promising eternal good fortune in such rich hunting grounds. The Plains tribes-men placed their dead on a kind of wooden scaffold, helping them on their way skywards. Much later, relatives would return to the spot and bury the bones.

Here we can see Chief **Horned Rock** who is very sad because someone close to him has died. In his grief he has torn out his hair and bandaged his head to cover the wounds. He has also had mystical symbols tattooed onto his neck, thus observing an age-old tradition.

Karl Bodmer was born in Zurich, Switzerland, on February 11, 1809. At the tender age of thirteen he began an apprenticeship as a landscape painter under his uncle, Johann Jakob Meyer, who also instructed Karl's elder brother Rudolf. As was common in those days, Karl set out as an itinerant artist in 1828 and traveled to the Rhineland region of Germany, where he sketched countless landscapes of the Rhine and the Mosel rivers. It was here that the naturalist and explorer Prince Maximilian of Wied was to discover this talented artist.

In 1832, Maximilian and Karl embarked on a trip to North America. On returning to Europe two years later with some 500 sketches and watercolors in his bags, the artist was given the nickname "Indian Bodmer." Illustrations based on the artist's pictures of America and its inhabitants appeared in Prince Maximilian's field journal, which was published several years later. Since it was in such great demand, the book was translated into both French and English. The latter is known under the title *Travels in the Interior of North America.*

Karl Bodmer was never to return to his friends in America. He was devastated when he heard the news that hit Europe a few years later: within a relatively short time, white man had wiped out nearly all Native Americans, either through his countless campaigns of destruction or by exposing the natives to new illnesses that proved fatal to them.

Later, Karl Bodmer moved to France where he found friends in the artists' colony in Barbizon, and turned his attention to painting animals. On October 30, 1893—nearly deaf and blind—Karl Bodmer died at the age of eighty-six. With his pictures of Native Americans, the artist left behind an invaluable legacy to the fascinating lives of America's first inhabitants. Most of the watercolors and drawings by the artist have come into the possession of the Joslyn Art Museum in Omaha, Nebraska, where they remain today.

This picture portrays one of the many occasions when the two travelers met a tribe of Native Americans. An interpreter is helping the two sides to communicate. Karl Bodmer can be seen on the far right with a big leather bag hanging from his shoulder in which he carried his painting materials. Prince Maximilian is on his left.